Universal Encyclopaedia of Excuses

Master the Art of Gracefully Getting Out of Anything

Table of contents

Introduction: The Fine Art of Excuse-Making

Let's face it—we've all been there. The moment you hear about your cousin's wedding, that text from a friend inviting you to dinner, or the ding of your calendar reminding you of an impending deadline at work. Suddenly, a wave of dread washes over you. You don't want to be there, do the thing, or handle the responsibility. But what can you do? Enter the noble art of excuse-making.

Excuses have been around for as long as humans have been expected to show up for stuff. But let me be clear—excuses are not lies (I mean, who are we? Villains?). Think of them as gentle evasions, clever deflections, or polite ways of saying, "No thanks, I'd rather do literally anything else."

This book is your toolkit. It's not for manipulating or deceiving anyone, but for gracefully dodging situations you just can't (or won't) handle. Whether you're bailing on a party or avoiding helping your cousin move (seriously, why do people even ask?), I've got your back with excuses for every occasion.

Now, without further ado, let's get started on your journey to becoming a master of the art of excuses. And remember, honesty is the best policy...unless you're being dragged to a three-hour meeting about nothing.

Work-Related Excuses—Because Sometimes, Netflix is Just More Important

Skipping a Meeting

Meetings are where productivity goes to die. Here's how to bow out gracefully when you simply can't handle yet another hour of pointless chatter.

1. **"Sorry, I have a conflicting call."** Translation: I'm going to mute my mic and watch YouTube videos of puppies for the next hour.

2. **"I'm dealing with a minor tech issue—can't seem to log in!"** Nothing brings sympathy quicker than the phrase "tech issue." No one will question it because everyone has been there. Plus, you can even throw in some jargon like "router failure" or "VPN problems" to make it extra convincing.

3. **"Got caught up in something urgent with a client."** Mysterious, vague, but sounds very important. This is the unicorn of meeting excuses because no one will ask for details. No one.

Missing a Deadline

So, you missed the deadline, huh? Happens to the best of us. Let's soften the blow with a well-crafted excuse.

1.   **"The file got corrupted, and I've been trying to retrieve it."** In the digital age, files getting corrupted is both a legitimate concern and a convenient scapegoat. The best part? It's completely unverifiable.

2.   **"I misunderstood the deadline. I thought it was next week!"** Innocent misunderstanding? Absolutely. Bonus points if you add, "But I'm almost done, just need a couple more hours."

3.   **"I've been dealing with a personal matter but didn't want to bother anyone with it."** This one makes you sound so noble and self-sacrificing that it's hard for anyone to be mad at you.

Avoiding Extra Work

Colleagues love to pass their work off on others. But you've got enough on your plate, right? Here's how to make sure you don't end up with their responsibilities.

1.	**"I'm swamped right now, but maybe next week?"** This buys you time, and most people forget they even asked after a week.

2.	**"I've been told to prioritize something else by my boss."** Name-drop your boss, and suddenly their request feels like a non-priority. Bonus: No one will argue with "upper management."

3.	**"I'm not really the best person for this task—maybe Sarah could help?"** Redirect their ask to another coworker who's better suited for the job... or just more willing to do it.

Taking a Day Off (When You Just Can't Even)

There's nothing like waking up and just knowing you won't make it through the day. You're in desperate need of a break, but how do you get one without looking lazy? Here's how.

1.   **"I've got a migraine coming on—I need to lie down."** No one questions the invisible illnesses. Migraines, in particular, are tricky to dispute and impossible to see. Perfect!

2.   **"I've got a personal emergency that just came up. I'll need to take the day off."** What constitutes a personal emergency? That's between you and your couch.

3.   **"I've been feeling under the weather. It's probably nothing, but I'd hate to risk bringing it into the office."** In the era of caution, this one works wonders. You're not only taking care of yourself but protecting your coworkers. How noble of you!

Leaving Work Early

Sometimes, you're simply done with the day by noon. You've been productive (or not), and it's time to bail.

1.   **"I've got a doctor's appointment that I couldn't reschedule."** Always believable, and no one wants to dig deeper into your medical history.

2.   **"I need to pick up a family member who's in a bit of a bind."** Family obligations are sacred ground. No one questions a family emergency.

3.   **"Something urgent came up with my pet."** The pet card is powerful. Whether it's an imagined vet visit or an escaped hamster, your coworkers will understand.

Calling in Sick

You're not actually sick, but boy, do you need a break. Time to craft the perfect "I'm too sick to work" excuse without sounding suspicious.

1.   **"I think I've caught that bug that's going around."** Ah, the generic, non-specific illness. No one can argue with a "bug," and it doesn't require further explanation.

2.   **"I've been up all night with a stomach issue—definitely not going to make it in today."** Stomach-related problems have the magic ability to make people stop asking questions immediately. Plus, they imply discomfort and helplessness—sympathy gold.

3.   **"I've been feeling feverish. I think it's best if I rest up today to avoid getting anyone else sick."** In the age of germs, this one works every time. You're responsible and considerate for staying away.

Avoiding a Business Trip

The idea of traveling for work can be exhausting before you even start packing. Here's how to make sure you're staying at home, guilt-free.

1.   **"I've got an important personal commitment that overlaps with the dates."** So vague, so unarguable. What's the commitment? Only you will ever know.

2.   **"I've been having some health concerns and my doctor advised me against traveling."** Nothing stops a business trip like doctor's orders. No one's going to demand a note.

3.   **"I don't think I'm the best fit for this trip, but I'd be happy to help prepare someone else."** Ah, delegating yourself right out of the trip while offering help? Genius.

Work is tough. But with these clever excuses, you can navigate the waters of professional life with a bit more grace and a lot less stress. Remember, the goal isn't to shirk all responsibilities, but to give yourself breathing room when you really need it. Keep these handy, and work-life balance might just feel a little more balanced.

Social Life Excuses—Because Sometimes, Your Couch is Your Best Friend

We all love our friends (well, most of them), but sometimes even the thought of putting on pants and interacting with other humans is exhausting. Whether it's skipping a party, dodging a blind date, or avoiding a family get-together, you need a social-life survival guide. Thankfully, I've got you covered with some perfectly reasonable and funny ways to get out of any social situation without causing too much drama.

Skipping a Party

You get the invite, and immediately your mind races with images of you curled up at home in your PJs instead. But how do you say no without looking like a total buzzkill?

1.   **"I'm so sorry, I've already got plans that night."** "Plans" could mean anything—from binging a new Netflix series to reorganizing your sock drawer. The beauty is in the vagueness. It's also a low-key way to let people down easily without getting too deep into the specifics.

2.   **"Ugh, I've come down with something. I don't want to spread it!"** People are extra cautious these days, and no one will want you near them if you even hint at feeling under the weather. Plus, it makes you seem thoughtful and responsible.

3.   **"I forgot I'm supposed to be dog-sitting for a friend, and the dog gets anxious when left alone for too long."**

Blame the dog! Pets are always great scapegoats, and no one questions the well-being of an anxious pup.

4.   **"I've been working late all week and I just need a night to recharge."** A solid excuse because everyone can relate to feeling worn out. Throw in a mention of "self-care," and your friends might even commend you for being so responsible with your mental health.

Missing a Family Reunion

Family reunions can be wonderful... unless they're not. Sometimes, they're an awkward mix of forced conversation and being reminded about how much everyone else is "achieving in life." Here's how to respectfully decline.

1.   **"I'm so sorry, I've got a work thing that I can't get out of."** Work is the universal excuse. Whether it's an actual work thing or just you needing to stay home, no one in the family will question a professional commitment.

2.   **"I've been feeling a bit off this week and don't want to risk spreading anything."** Again, health-related excuses are bulletproof. Family will appreciate you not bringing germs into the mix.

3.   **"I promised a friend I'd help them move, and I just can't bail."** Who can argue with a good deed? You're out there being a good friend, and it's hard to guilt-trip someone

for that. Plus, people know moving is a nightmare, so they might feel sorry for you instead.

Avoiding a Night Out

Some nights, you just don't have the energy to be social. Whether it's hitting up a bar, a fancy dinner, or a late-night event, here's how to bow out gracefully.

1.   **"I've had the longest day and am totally wiped out. I'd love to join next time!"** Blame the day, not the event. This lets you gently suggest that it's not the company that's the problem—it's just exhaustion. And who's going to argue with a tired person?

2.   **"I just remembered I have an early morning tomorrow. I'll have to pass this time."** The "early morning" excuse works like a charm, especially if it's vague enough to apply to anything from an appointment to an imaginary fitness class.

3.   **"I've got this nagging headache that just won't quit. I'm going to take it easy tonight."** Health again! Headaches are impossible to prove but entirely relatable.

People will wish you well and give you a free pass.

4.   **"I'm in the middle of a new book/show, and I just can't tear myself away."** A little honesty never hurt anyone. If your friends are chill, they'll totally understand needing a night of solo entertainment.

Dodging a Blind Date

Oh, the dreaded blind date. Maybe you agreed to it but are now filled with regret, or maybe your friends are pressuring you into one. Here's how to tap out without breaking too many hearts.

1.   **"I'm so sorry, but something urgent came up at work. I'll have to reschedule."** Again, work to the rescue. No one will argue with job commitments, and if you don't reschedule, well, that's a problem for future you.

2.   **"I've got a family thing I forgot about! Timing is just awful."** The key here is being vague enough that you don't have to explain further. "Family thing" could mean anything from helping someone out to avoiding the date altogether.

3.   **"I'm really not feeling great today, and I wouldn't want to be lousy company."** Health strikes again. No one

wants to date someone who's sick. You'll come off as thoughtful for putting their comfort above your own.

4.   **"I've been so swamped with stuff lately, I just don't think I'd be good company right now."** This makes it seem like you're doing them a favor by not bringing your stress into the date. Generous, no?

Bailing on Brunch or Dinner Plans

You agreed to brunch, but now that it's here, it seems like a terrible idea. Here's how to bail with minimal guilt.

1. **"I woke up with a sore throat. I don't think it's anything, but I'd rather be safe than sorry."** Self-care strikes again! Sore throats are just uncomfortable enough that no one will want to be near you, but not so serious that anyone would worry.

2. **"I completely forgot I promised to help my neighbor with something. They're moving, and I can't back out now."** The moving excuse is like the universal code for "I don't want to go." Everyone knows helping someone move is a miserable experience, so they'll immediately empathize and let you off the hook.

3. **"I've got a last-minute errand that just came up. Can we rain check?"** Last-minute stuff happens! By using "rain

check," you suggest that you genuinely want to reschedule, even if it's not true.

4.   **"I'm so tired today—I wouldn't be much fun. How about we reschedule for a time when I'm more lively?"** This is perfect for those days when you're feeling especially low-energy but still want to sound like you're keeping your friends' enjoyment in mind.

Ignoring a Phone Call or Message

The phone rings, and you immediately think, Not today, Satan. Or you've seen a message but just can't muster the energy to respond right away. Here's how to explain your lack of response without offending anyone.

1. **"I'm so sorry, I've been swamped all day and didn't have a chance to get back to you!"** Swamped? So relatable. Everyone's been there, and no one will hold it against you.

2. **"I saw your message and meant to respond, but I got distracted. Let's catch up soon!"** Blame distractions! In today's world of a million notifications, no one will be shocked that you lost track of time.

3. **"I was in the middle of something important and completely forgot to respond—my bad!"** This one is lighthearted and casual. You're not making excuses, you're just human!

4.   **"I've been really trying to unplug lately and take some time away from my phone. Let's chat soon!"** Throw in a little wellness angle. Everyone's striving for that perfect work-life balance, right? You're just being responsible with your screen time.

Your social life is supposed to be fun, but that doesn't mean you have to be on-call 24/7. These excuses will help you gracefully sidestep those moments when social obligations just feel like too much. The key is to be polite, a little vague, and always leave the door open for "next time." You'll stay on good terms with everyone while carving out the alone time you need (or avoiding that awkward blind date altogether).

Family Obligations—Because Sometimes You Just Can't Handle Aunt Susan's Stories

Family—where would we be without them? While we love them (most of the time), family events and obligations can feel like a never-ending loop of uncomfortable conversations, unsolicited advice, and the occasional heated political debate. Sometimes, you just need a little break from the madness. Whether it's skipping a family dinner, avoiding that cousin's wedding, or dodging an entire reunion, here are some tactful excuses that will keep the peace while letting you reclaim your sanity.

Skipping a Family Dinner

Family dinners are a staple of togetherness, but sometimes you're just not up for a round of "Why haven't you settled down yet?" or listening to Uncle Bob's latest conspiracy theory. Here's how to politely dodge without sounding like the family black sheep.

1.   **"I've had a crazy week at work and just need some time to unwind. Rain check?"** The "crazy workweek" card works every time. Everyone's been overwhelmed by work at some point, and no one can argue with your need to decompress.

2.   **"I've been feeling a little under the weather—don't want to risk passing anything along."** Again, health is your golden ticket. Family will appreciate your "concern" for their well-being, even if you're really just avoiding small talk.

3.   **"I've got an unexpected work call that I can't miss."** The beauty of the

unexpected work call is that no one can predict it, not even you! It's an easy out, and people usually respect work emergencies.

4.   **"I've been so tired lately—I think I'm just going to stay in and catch up on sleep tonight."** Fatigue is your friend. No one's going to force you to come over when you're already claiming exhaustion.

Avoiding Helping a Family Member Move

Family members helping each other move is basically a rite of passage. But carrying boxes, packing up kitchens, and navigating impossible stairwells? Not exactly a fun Saturday afternoon. Here's how to escape this grueling task while still sounding helpful.

1.   **"I've got a bad back—I wouldn't want to slow anyone down or injure myself further."** A bad back is the perfect physical excuse. Moving is hard work, and people won't want you to hurt yourself.

2.   **"I've got a work deadline I can't ignore, but I'd be happy to help you another way, like organizing!"** Offer an alternative that's less physically taxing. Helping to organize afterward is the kind of non-labor-intensive support that sounds helpful, but keeps you far away from the heavy lifting.

3.   **"I've got a prior commitment that day. Is there any way I can help another time?"** The prior commitment excuse is versatile—it can be anything from a non-negotiable appointment to "I promised to spend time with my dog."

4.   **"I've been fighting off a cold, and I don't want to risk being around everyone while I'm contagious."** Even if you're not actively sick, the mere mention of a potential illness is enough to keep you out of any group activity—especially something as physically involved as moving.

Skipping a Sibling's Event

Your sibling's big events—whether it's a recital, a school play, or yet another birthday party—can be fun, but sometimes you're just not in the mood. Here's how to gracefully skip out without being the "bad sibling."

1. **"I've been completely overwhelmed with work/school, and I just can't make it. I'll make it up to you!"** Work or school stress is a catch-all excuse that no one can argue with, especially if you throw in a promise to "make it up" later. A raincheck always softens the blow.

2. **"I've got an important commitment I can't move, but I'll be thinking of you!"** Your important commitment can be anything you want—gym class, a friend's event, or maybe even just a date with your couch. What matters is your intention.

3.   **"I'm really not feeling well today, and I'd hate to miss it, but I don't want to be a downer."** The health excuse strikes again! Not only do you come off as concerned about spreading germs, but you're also "sad" to be missing out. Win-win.

4.   **"I'm so sorry, I've got something that popped up last-minute. Let's celebrate together another day!"** When in doubt, the classic "last-minute pop-up" is vague enough to use anytime, and it keeps the door open for future fun.

Dodging a Family Reunion

Family reunions can be heartwarming... or completely overwhelming. Sometimes you just need to avoid all those relatives asking you life's most annoying questions: "When are you getting married?" "What do you do for a living again?" Here's how to dodge the reunion without causing a family scandal.

1.   **"I've got a work trip that weekend. Bad timing!"** Work to the rescue! Whether it's real or imaginary, a "work trip" gives you the perfect reason to miss the event. It's respectable, professional, and virtually unchallenged.

2.   **"I'm so sorry, I've had something booked for that weekend for months—I can't cancel now."** The long-standing commitment excuse works like a charm. The earlier you drop this one, the more believable it becomes. "Oh, I would've loved to come, but I've been locked into this for ages!"

3.   **"I've been under the weather and don't want to bring anything to the gathering."** Yet another health-related exit plan. Sick? No one will want you there, even if you claim it's just the sniffles. Stay home with your dignity intact.

4.   **"I've got a personal emergency that came up, and I won't be able to make it."** A personal emergency is perfect because it sounds serious enough that people won't pry, and it gets you out of the event completely guilt-free.

Avoiding Babysitting or Childcare Duties

Family members often assume you'll jump at the chance to babysit or help with the kids. But sometimes, you'd rather do...anything else. Here's how to say no without coming across as heartless.

1. **"I'd love to help, but I've got a ton of work to catch up on this weekend."** Work. Always work. A "ton of work" is vague, endless, and the perfect excuse to avoid long hours of childcare.

2. **"I'm not feeling 100%, and I wouldn't want to risk getting the kids sick."** No parent will want a potentially contagious babysitter around their children. You're just being considerate!

3. **"I've got plans that I can't back out of. Maybe next time?"** "Plans" can range from dinner with friends to catching up on

your favorite TV show. As long as they're unmovable, you're off the hook.

4.	**"I've been so stressed lately, I really need a weekend to myself to recharge."** Parents get it. Needing "me time" is relatable, and most will understand that you can't give your full attention to the kids if you're burnt out.

Skipping a Visit to Relatives

Sometimes, that weekend visit to Grandma's house, or spending the afternoon with relatives you barely know, just isn't in the cards. Here's how to politely get out of it without ruffling feathers.

1.   **"I've got a work deadline I really need to hit, so I'll have to pass this time."** The work deadline—your trusty, go-to excuse. It's believable and makes you look responsible, even if that "deadline" is just watching the entire season of your favorite show.

2.   **"I've had some unexpected car trouble, and I'm not sure I'll be able to make it."** The car is the perfect excuse—whether it's a flat tire, a dead battery, or just needing an "urgent" trip to the mechanic. It buys you time and sympathy.

3.   **"I've been so run down lately, I think I'll need to rest this weekend. Sorry!"** Fatigue is a powerful excuse.

Everyone needs rest, and no one will argue against you taking time to recharge.

4. **"I've got a personal commitment that I can't move. I'll make it up to you!"** A personal commitment could be anything—from attending a friend's event to going on a quiet solo retreat. Either way, it's unmovable and impossible to argue against.

Family is important, but so is your sanity! These excuses will help you navigate the often tricky terrain of family obligations without hurting anyone's feelings or getting sucked into something you really don't want to do. The trick is to be empathetic and thoughtful, even when you're planning to do exactly the opposite of what's being asked. With these in your arsenal, you can stay connected to your family—on your terms.

Romantic and Relationship Escapes—Because Love Doesn't Mean Always Saying "Yes"

Relationships are wonderful, but let's be real—sometimes, you just need a break from the endless couple activities, deep conversations, or hanging out with your partner's family. Whether it's dodging a date night, skipping a serious relationship talk, or avoiding meeting the in-laws (again), we've all been there. Luckily, there are some artful ways to get out of these situations without making your partner feel neglected. Here are some light-hearted and compassionate excuses for those times when you just need a little *me* time.

Skipping Date Night

As much as you adore spending time with your partner, sometimes you'd rather binge a show in your sweats than put on real clothes and go out. Here's how to lovingly bow out of date night without making it seem like you're uninterested.

1. **"I've had such a long day—can we reschedule for another night? I don't want to be lousy company."** Tiredness is universally relatable. Framing it as concern for your partner's experience makes you look thoughtful rather than lazy.

2. **"I think I'm coming down with something. I'd hate to get you sick!"** Ah, the classic "I'm not feeling well." It's thoughtful, considerate, and keeps you from having to dress up and leave the house. Plus, no one wants to be around someone who might be sick!

3.   **"I forgot I have an early start tomorrow—maybe we can do something low-key at home instead?"** The early start excuse is perfect because it shows you're responsible, but you're still offering to spend time together—just in a cozier setting that involves pajamas.

4.   **"I've been super stressed this week. Could we have a quiet night in instead? I'm just not up for going out."** Honesty with a sprinkle of vulnerability. Suggesting an alternative that still includes your partner shows you care, but also that you need to recharge.

Avoiding a Serious Conversation

Sometimes, you can feel that serious "relationship talk" coming. Whether you're just not in the headspace for it or you'd prefer to save it for later, here's how to hit pause without seeming like you're avoiding the issue (even if you are).

1. **"I really want to have this conversation, but I'm so drained today. Can we talk when I'm in a better place mentally?"** You're not saying no—you're saying *not now*. And framing it as needing to be in the right headspace makes it clear you want the talk to be productive, not stressful.

2. **"I think we should wait until we're both less tired/stressed. I want to make sure we give this conversation the attention it deserves."** This is perfect because it makes you sound considerate of the *quality* of the conversation. You're delaying out of respect for the topic, not dodging it.

3.   **"I've been feeling really anxious about work/family/something else today. I want to talk, but can we revisit this when I'm not so distracted?"** Anxiety and stress are real, and any empathetic partner will understand if you're not in the right emotional space for a serious discussion.

4.   **"I want to hear you out properly, but my mind is all over the place today. Let's set aside time tomorrow when I can focus better."** This conveys that you care about what they're saying, but you want to ensure you're giving them your full attention when you're in the right frame of mind.

Dodging Meeting the In-Laws (Again)

You've already met your partner's family, and it was...fine. But now you're being asked to spend yet *another* Saturday with them, and you just don't have the energy. Here's how to tactfully excuse yourself without causing a family rift.

1.   **"I've got a work deadline coming up, and I really need to focus this weekend. How about you go, and we'll plan something for just us soon?"** Work always works. This excuse not only gets you out of family time but also suggests quality time with your partner as a bonus.

2.   **"I've been feeling really run down, and I don't want to be bad company. You go ahead, and I'll rest up."** By positioning yourself as the one who'd bring down the mood, you make it easier for your partner to go solo without feeling guilty.

3.   **"I think I need to take care of some things around the house this weekend,**

but you should definitely go and enjoy!" This excuse makes it sound like you're being responsible and taking care of necessary things while subtly avoiding the family drama. Win-win!

4. **"I've been so overwhelmed with everything lately, I think I just need some time to myself to recharge. Why don't you go without me this time?"** The self-care card. Needing personal time to recharge is a perfectly acceptable reason to sit out a family gathering—especially if you position it as you wanting to be your best self when you do meet up again.

Skipping Couple's Therapy or a Relationship Retreat

Let's be real, sometimes even the most committed partners aren't in the mood for a relationship deep dive. Whether it's couple's therapy or a weekend retreat, here's how to bow out gracefully (at least for now).

1.   **"I've been feeling overwhelmed with everything going on—I don't think I'd be fully present. Can we reschedule?"** This excuse is about timing. It shows that you're not rejecting the idea but that you want to make sure it happens when you can give it your all.

2.   **"I think we're both a little burnt out right now. Maybe we should take a break and revisit this when we're both more refreshed."** You're framing it as something you want to do, but only when you can both benefit from it. It's about quality over quantity!

3.   **"I've had a rough week, and I really need some time to de-stress before diving into anything serious. Could we hold off until I'm in a better mindset?"** This is another variation of needing to be in the right headspace. You're still committed to the process—just not *today*.

4.   **"I'm really anxious about this. I know it's important, but can we take it slow and maybe not jump into a full retreat right now?"** By admitting you're feeling a bit overwhelmed, you make the request for delay more relatable and understandable.

Avoiding a Romantic Gesture When You're Just Not Feeling It

We've all been there. Your partner is in the mood for romance, but you're just…not. Whether it's an elaborate date or even something as small as cuddling, sometimes you need a way out that won't hurt anyone's feelings.

1. **"I've had a long day, and I'm not really in the right headspace for anything romantic tonight. Let's plan something for the weekend?"** You're pushing the romance to another day when you'll (hopefully) be more up for it, and it shows you still care.

2. **"I love that you're feeling romantic, but I'm feeling a little off tonight. How about we just chill together?"** This lets your partner know that while you're not up for grand gestures, you still

want to spend time together—just in a more relaxed way.

3.   **"I'm super tired, and I don't think I'll be any fun tonight. Can we raincheck for a time when I'm feeling more energized?"** Fatigue always works as a gentle excuse, especially when paired with a promise of future energy.

4.   **"I've been really stressed out and can't seem to get into a romantic mindset. I'd hate to ruin the mood—maybe we can try again tomorrow?"** Honesty about stress and needing to unwind is understandable and helps explain why you're not in the mood without hurting anyone's feelings.

Love and relationships are all about compromise, but that doesn't mean you can't occasionally take a step back to recharge. Whether it's skipping a date night, avoiding another family gathering, or postponing a serious conversation, these excuses will help you navigate relationship moments with empathy and tact. After all, a little time apart makes the heart grow fonder—right?

Fitness and Health Excuses—Because Sometimes the Couch is Calling Louder than the Gym

We all know that taking care of our bodies is important, but let's be honest—some days, getting out of bed and into workout clothes feels like scaling Mount Everest. Whether it's skipping the gym, dodging a hiking invite, or pretending you forgot about that yoga class you signed up for, everyone needs a good excuse to get out of physical activity once in a while. Here's how to do it without sacrificing your reputation as someone who "totally works out."

Skipping the Gym

There's a time and a place for the gym, and sometimes that time is never. When you've promised yourself (or someone else) that you'll go, but you just can't bring yourself to do it, here are some graceful ways to back out.

1.   **"I woke up with a killer headache. I don't think I can make it today."** Headaches are the perfect excuse for skipping a workout—they're invisible, and no one questions your discomfort. Plus, cardio + headache = nightmare.

2.   **"I pulled a muscle last time I worked out. Better rest it today!"** No one argues with injury prevention. This excuse keeps you safely on the couch while sounding responsible about your long-term fitness goals.

3.   **"I forgot I had a work call right in the middle of my workout window. Looks like I'll have to reschedule."** Work strikes again! People love a good work-related

excuse, and no one's going to make you choose squats over your job.

4.   **"I'm feeling a bit run down today. I don't want to overdo it and make things worse."** Being cautious about your health makes you sound responsible. Plus, who wants to risk feeling worse after dragging themselves to the gym?

Avoiding a Hike or Outdoor Activity

Ah, the invitation to hike. It sounds great in theory—fresh air, exercise, nature—but in reality, it often means sweating, bugs, and sore legs. When you'd rather stay in a temperature-controlled environment, here's how to politely decline.

1.   **"I'm still recovering from my last workout. I don't think my legs could handle a hike today!"** This excuse works wonders because it shows you're active...just not today. You've already "done the work," so no one can fault you for needing a break.

2.   **"I've got a ton of errands to run this weekend. I won't be able to make it this time."** Errands are vague, never-ending, and somehow always believable. No one's going to argue with your busy schedule.

3.   **"The weather's not looking great. I wouldn't want us to get caught in the rain!"** Blaming the weather is perfect because

it's completely out of your control. Plus, no one wants to trudge through mud or get drenched halfway up a mountain.

4.   **"I've been dealing with some foot pain lately. I don't think a hike is the best idea right now."** Foot pain (or any pain, really) is a go-to for avoiding anything that involves walking. You're "protecting your future fitness" by skipping out today.

Dodging a Fitness Class

Whether it's spin class, yoga, or that new HIIT session you thought was a good idea at the time, sometimes you just don't feel like going. Here's how to get out of it without admitting you'd rather binge-watch Netflix.

1. **"I completely forgot I had a dentist/doctor's appointment today. I'll have to miss the class."** Appointments are excellent excuses because they're important, unavoidable, and no one will press you for details.

2. **"I didn't sleep well last night, and I don't want to risk pushing myself too hard today."** Being mindful of your limits makes you sound responsible, not lazy. Plus, who's going to argue with the need for more sleep?

3. **"I think I'm coming down with something, and I'd hate to spread it around the class."** Health and hygiene are

top priorities these days, and no one will want you in a class if you even hint at being sick.

4.   **"I got caught up at work and won't be able to make it in time. Let's try again next week!"** Work to the rescue! Being a little too busy is a valid excuse that still makes you sound like a productive adult.

Saying No to a Group Run or Marathon Training

The thought of running a marathon sounds inspiring...until it actually comes time to train. If you've committed to a run with friends but are now rethinking your life choices, here's how to get out of it.

1.   **"I've been dealing with some knee pain, so I think I need to rest instead of run."** Knee pain is the ultimate runner's excuse—legitimate, relatable, and serious enough to avoid questions. No one wants to see you push through an injury.

2.   **"I didn't hydrate properly today, and I'd hate to risk feeling faint during the run."** Not hydrating enough is a pro-level excuse because it's both specific and health-conscious. Plus, it's a good reminder to your friends that safety comes first.

3.   **"I've got a huge project deadline, and I really can't take time off work right**

now. Let's run next weekend!" Work, work, work. No one can argue with your priorities, and you buy yourself another week of freedom.

4.   **"I've been feeling really off this week. I think I'd be more of a hindrance than a help to the group today."** Framing it as you not wanting to hold the group back makes you seem selfless, even if you just want to avoid all that cardio.

Avoiding a "Healthy" Group Activity (Juice Cleanses, Meditation Retreats, etc.)

Every now and then, you'll be invited to join a group doing something "healthy" that just sounds...awful. Whether it's a weekend meditation retreat or a juice cleanse that promises to "cleanse your soul," here's how to bow out gracefully.

1. **"I've been dealing with some digestive issues lately, so a juice cleanse might not be the best idea for me."** No one is going to argue with digestive health. It's the kind of excuse that makes everyone back away quickly while wishing you well.

2. **"I love the idea, but I've already got something planned for that weekend. Maybe next time?"** A prior engagement is a solid, guilt-free way to get out of anything. Plus, it leaves room for you to

"maybe" join next time (but that's future you's problem).

3.   **"I've been feeling really stressed out, and I think what I need most right now is some time to rest on my own."** Even for a meditation retreat, this excuse works. You're acknowledging the stress but explaining that solo time is what you really need right now.

4.   **"I've got some dietary restrictions, and I'm not sure the cleanse/retreat would work for me."** Dietary restrictions (real or imagined) are a fantastic excuse for avoiding any food-related activity. No one's going to push you to do something that could make you uncomfortable.

Fitness is important, but so is knowing when you need a break. These excuses will help you gracefully dodge those times when working out, hiking, or attending that 5 a.m. yoga class just isn't happening. You'll keep your reputation as a health-conscious individual while also keeping your couch company for just a little longer. After all, balance is key, right?

Financial and Favor Dodging—Because Sometimes You Just Can't (or Don't Want to) Open Your Wallet

Money makes the world go 'round, but sometimes you just don't feel like spending yours. Whether you're being asked to lend money, chip in for a group gift, or donate to a cause, there's always that moment where you think, *Do I really have to?* And then there are those favors—helping someone move, babysitting, or doing someone else's chores—that make you wonder, *Why did I say yes to this?* Here's how to dodge financial asks and favors without feeling like a Scrooge or a bad friend.

Dodging Lending Money to Friends or Family

Nothing strains relationships faster than money. Whether it's your buddy needing a quick loan or a family member asking for "just a little help," lending money can get awkward—fast. Here's how to politely decline without burning bridges.

1.   **"I'd love to help, but things are a bit tight for me right now."** The classic "money's tight" excuse works because it's believable and relatable. Whether you're actually saving up for something or just don't want to hand over cash, this one says, "I get it, but I can't."

2.   **"I've already committed to a few other expenses this month. Maybe next time?"** This is a softer approach—you're explaining that your finances are already spoken for, but you're leaving the door open for

potential help in the future (even if you don't plan to follow up on that).

3.   **"I try to avoid lending money to friends or family because I've seen it cause issues in the past. I hope you understand!"** Honesty, wrapped in a little life lesson. This excuse subtly frames lending money as a potential relationship risk, making it hard for the other person to argue without seeming unreasonable.

4.   **"I've been trying to stick to a strict budget lately, so I don't have much flexibility. I hope you can find some help elsewhere."** Budgeting—nobody questions a strict budget! It makes you sound responsible, and most people won't push you when you say you're trying to save.

Skipping Contributing to Group Gifts or Donations

It's great to chip in for gifts and charitable causes...until the fifth person asks you to do it in the same month. If your wallet is starting to feel the strain, here's how to respectfully bow out.

1.   **"I've already donated to a few causes this month, so I'll have to pass on this one. But I wish you guys the best!"** This one shows that you're still generous but simply tapped out from previous donations. It's thoughtful and gives you a break without seeming stingy.

2.   **"I'm saving up for something right now, so I need to watch my spending. Sorry I can't contribute this time!"** Whether you're saving for a real goal or just watching your spending in general, this excuse works well for group gifts and donations without causing guilt.

3.   **"I'd love to help, but I'm on a tight budget this month. Hopefully, next time I can chip in!"** It's honest, and the mention of "next time" keeps you on good terms with the group without committing to anything in the moment.

4.   **"I've already got some financial commitments this month, so I'll have to pass. I hope the event goes well!"** Prior commitments are a great way to say no without shutting the door completely. Whether it's bills, savings, or just treating yourself, no one needs to know the details!

Dodging a Request to Help Someone Move

Ah, moving—the ultimate favor. No one *wants* to spend their Saturday lifting heavy boxes, yet somehow, we all get roped into it at some point. If you'd rather do literally anything else, here's how to decline with finesse.

1. **"I've been dealing with some back pain lately, and I wouldn't want to make it worse."** The classic "bad back" excuse is timeless. No one will expect you to lift boxes if you mention any kind of physical discomfort—better safe than sorry!

2. **"I've already got plans that day, but I'd love to help you unpack later!"** You're busy (even if "busy" means a Netflix marathon), but you're still offering to help out in a less physically demanding way. This keeps you in the good books without committing to the heavy lifting.

3.   **"I've got a work project I need to finish up, so I won't be able to help. I hope the move goes smoothly!"** Work is a wonderful excuse because it's serious and unarguable. Plus, it gives you an out while wishing them well—very classy.

4.   **"I'd love to help, but I've got a family thing that weekend. Let me know how it goes!"** Family obligations are the kind of excuse no one challenges. It's vague enough to be believable without needing further details.

Avoiding Being the "Designated Helper" for Chores

There's always that one person who asks for help with chores—whether it's mowing the lawn, assembling furniture, or fixing something around the house. If you'd rather not spend your Saturday doing someone else's to-do list, here's how to politely back out.

1. **"I've been swamped with my own projects lately, so I'm afraid I won't have time this weekend."** A little truth mixed with a little excuse. You've got your own stuff going on—who can argue with that?

2. **"I've got a bunch of errands to run this weekend, so I'll be tied up. Maybe I can help another time."** Errands are the perfect excuse because they're time-consuming, boring, and a surefire way to avoid extra tasks. Just make sure your schedule sounds full!

3. **"I've been meaning to tackle some stuff at home myself, so I'll need to focus**

on that. Good luck!" This one's great because you're not just avoiding their chores—you're prioritizing your own. It sounds responsible and gets you off the hook.

4. **"I'm afraid I've got other commitments this weekend, but maybe you can ask [insert another friend's name]?"** Offering another person (as long as they're not within earshot) is a clever way to redirect the ask while avoiding the chore yourself.

Skipping Helping a Friend with a Major Purchase (like a Car or House)

When someone asks you to help with a big financial decision—like buying a car or house—it can feel like a lot of pressure. Maybe you're not comfortable giving advice, or maybe you just don't want to get involved. Here's how to decline without seeming unhelpful.

1.	**"I'm really not an expert on this, so I don't think I'd be much help. Maybe you could talk to someone who knows more about it?"** Admitting you're out of your depth is both honest and gets you off the hook. Plus, you're directing them to someone who might actually know what they're talking about!

2.	**"I've got a really busy week coming up, so I don't think I can help right now. I hope it goes well, though!"** Blame a packed schedule, and your friend will probably understand. You're still wishing them the best, but just don't have the bandwidth for it.

3. **"I'm not really comfortable giving advice on something this big. I wouldn't want to steer you wrong."** This is perfect for avoiding major decisions—whether financial or otherwise. It's thoughtful because you're acknowledging the importance of the choice and stepping out of the way.

4. **"I've got a lot going on right now, so I'm afraid I can't take the time to help. But I'm sure you'll make a great choice!"** Another gentle way to bow out. You're giving your support without getting tangled up in the details.

Finances and favors are tricky to navigate, but with these excuses, you can politely avoid situations that strain your wallet or your time. The key is to strike the right balance between being helpful and setting boundaries. You don't have to be everyone's ATM or personal assistant—these excuses will help you keep your peace of mind (and your Saturday afternoons) intact. Just remember: It's okay to say no!

Public and Formal Commitments—Because Sometimes Obligations Aren't as Fun as They Sound

Formal events and public commitments have a way of sneaking up on you—weddings, funerals, charity events, and even jury duty. Sure, they're important, but sometimes they come at a time when you'd rather be anywhere else. Whether it's attending a friend's big day, showing up for a charity fundraiser, or facing the prospect of sitting through jury duty, here's how to respectfully decline or delay your participation without offending anyone or shirking your civic duties.

Skipping a Wedding

Weddings are beautiful, but sometimes they're also expensive, far away, or just not your cup of tea. Here's how to skip out on a wedding (even if you RSVP'd "yes") without making the bride and groom feel slighted.

1. **"I'm so sorry, but something urgent came up at work that weekend. I won't be able to make it, but I'll definitely send my best wishes!"** Work strikes again! It's the go-to excuse for backing out of anything last-minute. You're still showing that you care, but something unavoidable has come up.

2. **"I've been feeling under the weather, and I'd hate to risk attending while I'm not 100%."** The health card—again, bulletproof. No one will want you to bring your germs to their wedding.

3. **"I just realized I have a prior commitment that I can't move. I'm so**

disappointed to miss it, but I'll be thinking of you!" Whether you're attending another event, visiting family, or staying in to relax, the key here is vagueness. You're expressing regret but keeping your excuse light.

4. **"I've had an unexpected family emergency and won't be able to attend. I hope it's a beautiful day, and I'll celebrate with you soon!"** Family emergencies are a top-tier excuse because they're serious and rarely questioned. Just make sure you express your sadness about missing the event.

Avoiding a Funeral

Funerals are important, but not everyone feels comfortable attending them—especially if the person was a distant relative or acquaintance. Here's how to respectfully decline without seeming indifferent.

1.   **"I'm so sorry, I've got a work obligation that I can't reschedule, but my thoughts are with the family."** Work is an excellent way out of many formal events. While it's important to pay respects, a work conflict is a strong and respectful excuse.

2.   **"I've been feeling unwell, and I wouldn't want to risk attending while I'm under the weather. My condolences to the family."** Health-related excuses work well here, as no one will want to catch whatever illness you're claiming to have.

3.   **"I'm really sorry, but I'm unable to attend due to a family commitment. I'll be sure to send my condolences."** A prior

family commitment is another safe excuse that won't offend anyone. It shows that you're still thoughtful, but you've got other pressing obligations.

4.   **"I'm not able to make it to the service, but I'll be sure to send a card to the family."** This one is simple but effective—you're acknowledging the importance of the event but finding another way to show your respect.

Bailing on a Charity Event

Charity events are great, but sometimes your calendar (or your mood) just doesn't match up with the invitation. Whether it's a gala, a fundraising walk, or a dinner, here's how to gracefully back out without looking like a bad person.

1.   **"I've got a work commitment that's come up, and I won't be able to attend. I'll make a donation to the cause, though!"** Offering to donate, even if you can't attend, is a great way to show support without actually showing up. Plus, work commitments are always a good reason to miss out.

2.   **"I've been dealing with some health issues and won't be able to make it. I hope the event goes well!"** Health issues strike again—always believable, always acceptable. Just make sure you wish them success.

3.   **"I've had a scheduling conflict come up and won't be able to make it, but I'd love to support the cause in other ways!"** By offering to help in a different capacity (like spreading the word or donating), you stay involved while getting out of the event.

4.   **"I completely forgot I'd already committed to something else that day. So sorry I'll miss it, but I hope the event is a huge success!"** Forgetting a prior commitment is a reasonable, human mistake—and people usually won't press for details. Just be sure to apologize sincerely!

Avoiding Jury Duty

Jury duty: it's our civic duty, but it's also often inconvenient and time-consuming. While it's not always easy to dodge this one, there are ways to buy yourself some time (or even get excused altogether).

1.   **"I'm dealing with some health issues that would make it difficult for me to serve right now. Is there a way to defer my service?"** Health issues (especially mental or physical conditions) are a legitimate reason to request a deferral or even an exemption. Just be sure to provide a doctor's note if required.

2.   **"I've got an important work project that would make it nearly impossible for me to serve at this time. Is it possible to defer my duty?"** Work commitments, especially if they involve deadlines or travel, can sometimes get you a

deferment. Just be ready to explain how critical your role is.

3.   **"I've got a family obligation that requires my attention during this time. Is there any way to reschedule my service?"** Family commitments are another potential reason for deferment. You're not shirking your duty—you're just requesting it at a more convenient time.

4.   **"I've already got a vacation planned and paid for. Can my jury duty be rescheduled for a later date?"** Prior travel plans, especially if they're non-refundable, can sometimes be a good reason to reschedule. Who doesn't sympathize with someone looking forward to their vacation?

Skipping a Graduation or School Event

Graduations are long, crowded, and often far away. Whether it's your cousin's high school graduation or your friend's child's ceremony, here's how to politely skip the hours of speeches and clapping.

1.   **"I'm so sorry, but I've got a prior work commitment I can't miss. I'll celebrate with you afterward!"** Work is always a believable reason to skip a formal event. Just make sure you follow up with congratulations later.

2.   **"I've got a family event that day, and I won't be able to make it to the graduation. I hope it's a wonderful celebration!"** A prior family obligation is a solid, respectful excuse. It's hard for people to argue with "family comes first."

3.   **"I've been feeling under the weather lately, so I'll have to sit this one**

out. But I'll be there in spirit!" Health, once again, is a great way to excuse yourself from crowded events. No one wants to be around someone who isn't feeling well.

4.   **"I'm afraid I won't be able to attend, but I'll be thinking of you and can't wait to hear how it goes!"** This is a soft and simple way to excuse yourself without going into too many details. You're offering support without showing up in person.

Dodging Being on a Committee or Board

Being asked to serve on a committee or board can feel like a huge compliment...until you realize how much time it's going to take. If you're not ready for the commitment, here's how to decline gracefully.

1. **"I'm so flattered by the offer, but I've got too much on my plate right now to give it the attention it deserves."** This is polite and flattering. You're acknowledging the honor but also making it clear that you don't want to overextend yourself.

2. **"I'd love to help, but I'm already committed to another project that's taking up most of my time. I'll have to pass this time around."** Other commitments—whether work, family, or personal—are always a valid reason to decline without sounding uninterested.

3.   **"I'm afraid my schedule won't allow for it right now, but I'd be happy to help in a different capacity if needed."** Offering to help in a smaller, less time-consuming way shows that you still care about the cause, even if you can't commit to the full role.

4.   **"I've been trying to focus on balancing my work and personal life, so I don't think I can take on any additional responsibilities at the moment."** Prioritizing work-life balance is something everyone can understand. It makes you sound responsible, not lazy.

Formal events and public commitments often feel like obligations we can't escape—but with the right excuse, you can bow out gracefully while still being polite and considerate. Whether it's a wedding, charity event, or even jury duty, these excuses will help you manage your time and commitments without offending anyone. Sometimes, it's okay to say no, and with these strategies, you'll do it in style.

School or Educational Excuses—Because Sometimes Studying is Optional

School is a place for learning, but let's be real—sometimes the idea of going to class or finishing an assignment just doesn't sit well with you. Whether you're a student trying to get out of a lecture, someone with a forgotten assignment, or a parent avoiding a parent-teacher conference, we all need an excuse here and there. Below, you'll find ways to dodge everything from group study sessions to homework submissions with finesse and maybe even a little humor.

Skipping a Class or Lecture

Classes are important, but there are days when attending feels like an impossible task—especially when it's a three-hour lecture on something that makes your brain melt. Here's how to respectfully avoid class without risking too much side-eye from your teacher or professor.

1.   **"I woke up feeling really unwell today, so I think it's best I rest. I'll catch up on the material later!"** Sick days work just as well in school as they do in the workplace. Plus, your dedication to catching up later shows responsibility (even if you're catching up on sleep instead).

2.   **"I've got a family emergency that I need to attend to. I'll make sure to go over the notes!"** The family emergency card is hard to argue with. It's vague, serious, and understandable without needing to explain the details.

3.   "I had an important appointment scheduled today that I couldn't miss. I'll review the lecture recording later!" Medical or personal appointments are great excuses because they're often non-negotiable. Just be sure to mention you'll stay on top of the material.

4.   "I've been feeling really burnt out lately, and I need a mental health day to recharge. I'll check in with the professor to catch up." Mental health days are becoming more recognized as legitimate reasons to miss class. A day off for self-care shows maturity and self-awareness.

Not Turning in an Assignment on Time

Oops. The deadline for that big paper or project came and went, and your work is nowhere near done. Don't panic! Here's how to buy yourself some extra time without admitting you completely forgot.

1.   **"I had some personal issues come up that prevented me from finishing the assignment. Could I have an extension?"** Personal issues are a broad, relatable excuse that no one is going to push you on. This approach usually buys you a few extra days with minimal fuss.

2.   **"My computer crashed, and I lost most of my work. I'm trying to recover the files but might need a bit more time."** The good ol' "tech issue" excuse. It's especially believable in today's digital age. Plus, it implies that you *were* working hard—until disaster struck.

3.   "I misunderstood the deadline—I thought it was next week. I'm almost done, but could I submit it tomorrow?" Simple confusion is one of the least confrontational excuses. A genuine misunderstanding of deadlines happens, and most instructors will be sympathetic.

4.   "I've been dealing with a lot of stress lately, and I wasn't able to focus on the assignment. Could I turn it in late with a small penalty?" Admitting that you've been under stress shows honesty, and most teachers will appreciate the maturity of owning up to needing more time—especially if you're willing to accept a small penalty.

Avoiding Group Study Sessions

Group study sessions can be helpful...or they can be a chaotic mess of everyone chatting and getting nothing done. If you'd rather study solo (or not at all), here's how to skip out on your study buddies.

1.   **"I've got a personal appointment that overlaps with the study session time. I'll have to miss it, but let me know if you cover anything important!"** Appointments are always a solid excuse. You're not rejecting the group—you just have a prior commitment that you can't change.

2.   **"I've been feeling really run down, and I don't want to bring everyone down. I'll study on my own this time."** Fatigue is relatable. By mentioning that you don't want to affect the group dynamic, you sound considerate while also carving out time for yourself.

3.   **"I study better on my own, but I'm happy to compare notes afterward!"** Sometimes, a simple truth works best. If group sessions aren't your thing, just own it—but still offer to stay involved by exchanging notes.

4.   **"I've got a family thing I need to take care of during that time. I'll catch up with you guys afterward!"** Family obligations are a perfect go-to for anything. They're serious, important, and rarely questioned.

Skipping a Parent-Teacher Conference

For parents, the idea of sitting down with your child's teacher can sometimes be more nerve-wracking than it needs to be. If you can't make it (or just don't want to), here's how to excuse yourself without seeming disinterested.

1.   **"I've got a work conflict and won't be able to attend the conference. Could we set up a time to chat over the phone?"** Work conflicts are always understandable, and offering an alternative (like a phone call) shows that you're still engaged, just not available at that moment.

2.   **"I've got a family emergency and won't be able to make it. I'll follow up with the teacher afterward."** Family emergencies are a rock-solid excuse for anything. Just be sure to follow through on your promise to check in later.

3.   **"I've been feeling unwell and don't want to risk attending in person. Could we reschedule?"** Illness is a legitimate reason to stay home, especially in today's climate. Teachers will understand, and rescheduling shows your commitment to the discussion.

4.   **"I've got a prior commitment that day, but I'd love to reschedule for another time."** Prior commitments are a respectful excuse, and most teachers are happy to accommodate rescheduling—especially if you give enough notice.

Avoiding School Volunteering or PTA Meetings

Volunteering at school or attending PTA meetings is great...in theory. But sometimes your calendar—or your sanity—just doesn't allow for it. Here's how to get out of those extra commitments while still looking like an involved parent.

1.   **"I'm sorry, but I've got a work deadline that I can't miss. Hopefully, I can help out next time!"** Work deadlines are always a valid excuse. You're still showing support, just not this time around.

2.   **"I've already committed to something else that day, but I'll be there in spirit!"** The classic "prior commitment" excuse works wonders here. Whether you're genuinely busy or just not in the mood, it's a guilt-free way to bow out.

3.   **"I've been feeling overwhelmed lately, and I don't think I can add**

anything else to my plate right now. I'll have to sit this one out." Being honest about feeling overwhelmed is relatable, and most people will respect your boundaries if you admit you need to take a step back.

4. **"I'm afraid I've got other family obligations that weekend. I hope the event goes well!"** Family obligations are another go-to for politely declining involvement. It's hard for people to argue with a family-first approach.

Not Completing Online Course Modules or Homework

Online courses and self-paced learning can be a great way to grow, but sometimes it's hard to keep up. If you've fallen behind on your online course or forgotten to submit that module quiz, here's how to explain yourself without getting too much heat.

1. **"I've been dealing with some unexpected personal issues, and I haven't been able to keep up with the modules. Is there any way to extend the deadlines?"** Personal issues are broad and often unquestioned, especially in online learning environments. Most instructors will grant extensions if asked politely.

2. **"I've had some tech problems with my computer, and I haven't been able to access the course properly. Could I get some extra time?"** Blaming technology is the perfect excuse for online coursework. Internet

issues, computer crashes, or even platform bugs all buy you a bit of extra time.

3.   **"I've had a really heavy workload lately, and I've fallen behind. Would it be possible to get an extension to catch up?"** Workload overwhelm is something everyone can relate to—whether it's your job, studies, or life in general. Most online programs are flexible and willing to help you stay on track.

4.   **"I've been dealing with a lot of stress and haven't been able to focus. Is there a way to get an extension on the assignments?"** Mental health is important, and most online courses recognize this. Explaining your stress is a reasonable way to ask for more time without guilt.

School and education can be stressful, but these excuses will help you navigate everything from skipping class to catching up on late assignments without burning bridges. The trick is to be respectful and clear while giving yourself the breathing room you need—whether that's for studying or for an extra Netflix binge. Remember, everyone needs a break sometimes, and these excuses will help you handle your educational commitments with grace.

Miscellaneous Excuses—Because Life is Full of Unexpected Obligations

There are always those random, miscellaneous situations in life that catch you off guard—an unexpected knock at the door, a survey request, or even those moments when you just don't feel like adulting. These scenarios don't fit neatly into categories, but that doesn't mean you can't dodge them with a clever excuse. From avoiding door-to-door salespeople to sidestepping jury duty questionnaires, here's how to handle the unexpected with style.

Not Answering the Door

Sometimes, you just don't want to deal with whoever is knocking at your door—whether it's a salesperson, a neighbor, or that family member who drops by unannounced. Here's how to get out of answering the door without looking rude.

1.   **"I didn't hear the doorbell; I must have been in the shower!"** The shower is a wonderful excuse because it's both true (in theory) and unverifiable. Plus, no one expects you to hop out of the shower to answer the door.

2.   **"Sorry, I was on an important work call and couldn't step away."** Work calls are a great way to avoid in-person interactions. Everyone respects someone who's busy with work, and this excuse makes it seem like you were being responsible.

3.   **"I was on the phone with a family member who needed me, so I couldn't**

answer the door at that moment." Family emergencies or even just family drama are excellent reasons for not being able to get to the door. It's a personal, non-controversial reason to be unavailable.

4. **"Oh no, I must have been out running errands! Sorry I missed you."** This excuse works well when you've ignored a knock at the door—just claim you weren't home. It's simple, believable, and gets you off the hook.

Avoiding Door-to-Door Salespeople

We've all been there—a knock at the door and a smiling salesperson trying to get you to buy something you don't want or need. Here's how to politely get out of the conversation without buying a vacuum cleaner.

1.   **"I'm sorry, but I'm really busy right now. I don't have time to chat."** Being "busy" is a great excuse for cutting the interaction short. Whether you're working, taking care of something important, or just pretending to be, this one works like a charm.

2.   **"I'm not interested, but thank you for stopping by."** Sometimes, a simple and polite "no thanks" is all you need. It's firm but kind, and it closes the conversation without dragging it out.

3.   **"I'm actually on a conference call right now—sorry I can't talk."** The conference call excuse makes you sound busy

and professional, giving you a quick out while still being polite.

4.   **"I've already got one of those, but thanks for offering!"** Claiming you already own the product they're selling is a clever way to get out of the pitch without looking disinterested. You're essentially saying, "I'm already a satisfied customer."

Skipping an Unwanted Survey or Feedback Request

Sometimes you're asked to fill out a survey or provide feedback on something you don't care about. If you'd rather not spend your time answering endless questions, here's how to get out of it.

1.   **"I'm sorry, but I'm really swamped with work and won't be able to complete the survey right now."** Being too busy is a solid excuse that no one can argue with. It's respectful and professional while giving you an easy out.

2.   **"I didn't receive the email link for the survey. Could you resend it?"** This stalling tactic works well if you're hoping they'll forget to follow up. By claiming you never received the link, you buy time without outright refusing.

3.   **"I've been dealing with a personal issue that's taking up most of my time,**

so I won't be able to participate in the survey." Personal issues (without giving too much detail) are a respectful excuse that most people will understand and not question.

4.   "I'm traveling and won't have access to my computer for a while, so I'll have to pass on the survey." Travel is always a great excuse to dodge online surveys. It's simple, believable, and gives you a polite reason to skip it altogether.

Dodging an Invitation to Speak or Present at an Event

Being asked to speak or present at an event is an honor... but sometimes you'd rather not deal with the stress, preparation, or public speaking. Here's how to politely decline without seeming ungrateful.

1. **"I'm so flattered by the invitation, but I've got a scheduling conflict and won't be able to participate."** This is a respectful and graceful way to say no without hurting anyone's feelings. You're honored, but busy!

2. **"I've been feeling really overwhelmed with work and personal commitments, so I won't be able to speak this time. I hope the event goes well!"** By mentioning that you're juggling too much, you express regret without sounding uninterested. It shows you care about the event, but just can't fit it in.

3.   **"I'm traveling during that time, so unfortunately, I'll have to decline the invitation."** Travel, especially if it's work-related, is a great reason to bow out of a speaking event. It's practical and impossible to argue with.

4.   **"I don't think I'll be able to contribute as much as I'd like due to other commitments, but I really appreciate the offer."** Sometimes it's best to admit that you won't be able to give the event your full attention. This sounds responsible and respectful while keeping the door open for future opportunities.

Getting Out of Attending a Book Club or Local Meetup

Book clubs, hobby meetups, or neighborhood gatherings can be fun...until you're not in the mood to socialize. If you've agreed to attend but now want to back out, here's how to excuse yourself without looking flaky.

1.   **"I've had something come up with work that I can't get out of. I'll catch up with you all next time!"** Work commitments are the perfect excuse for skipping out on low-stakes social gatherings. It's believable and professional.

2.   **"I've been feeling a little under the weather, so I'll have to miss this one. I hope you all have fun!"** Health excuses always work for small group meetups. No one wants to be around someone who might be sick, so you're doing them a favor.

3.   **"I completely forgot I have another appointment scheduled for that day. So**

sorry I won't make it!" Forgetting about a prior commitment is a human mistake and an easy way out of a casual group event. Apologize, and most people will understand.

4. **"I've been really overwhelmed lately, and I think I need to take a break and recharge. Hopefully, I can join next time!"** Prioritizing mental health is a valid excuse for skipping any social event. Everyone understands the need to recharge from time to time.

Avoiding Grocery Shopping

There's nothing inherently wrong with grocery shopping, except when it's your turn to do it, and you're just not feeling it. If someone's asking you to run to the store, but the thought of it makes you want to crawl back into bed, here's how to dodge the trip.

1.   **"I'm swamped with work today—I won't have time to run to the store. Can we order delivery instead?"** Blame work, then suggest a convenient alternative that doesn't involve you stepping foot outside. Grocery delivery is a great way to sound helpful while staying put.

2.   **"I'm not feeling great, and I'd hate to risk going out and making it worse. Could we put it off until tomorrow?"** Feeling a little off is a perfect excuse for avoiding public places. Most people won't want you dragging yourself around the grocery store if you're unwell.

3.   **"The car's acting up, and I don't think it's a good idea to drive right now. Maybe we can figure out another way to get what we need?"** Car trouble is the ultimate "get out of errands free" card. Plus, it's hard to argue with safety concerns when it comes to transportation.

4.   **"I've got a really tight schedule today. Do we really need the groceries right now, or can it wait?"** Sometimes all you need is to plant the idea of postponement. Once the urgency of the task is questioned, people may realize that it's not so necessary after all.

Skipping Home Repairs

Home repairs are one of those things that are always there but never convenient. When your spouse or housemate suggests that now is the perfect time to fix that leaky faucet, broken shelf, or squeaky door, but you're just not in the mood, here's how to get out of it.

1.   **"I've been having some back pain, and I don't want to make it worse by lifting anything heavy or bending too much."** Physical discomfort is always a reliable way to avoid manual labor. No one wants to be responsible for aggravating an injury.

2.   **"I've got an important deadline coming up, and I can't afford to take time away from work right now. Maybe we can tackle it this weekend?"** Work to the rescue again! This excuse buys you more time and shifts the focus away from the task for now.

3.   **"I think we'll need a professional for this one. I'm not sure I have the right tools, and I wouldn't want to mess it up."** Admitting that a task might be beyond your expertise is a great way to avoid doing it yourself. Plus, no one wants to risk making things worse by DIY-ing beyond their skill level.

4.   **"I've had a really stressful week and just need some time to unwind. Maybe we can look at it later when I'm feeling up to it."** Mental fatigue is a perfectly valid excuse for not diving into home repairs. Stress reduction comes first, right?

Ignoring Household Projects

There's always some project looming in the background—whether it's repainting a room, organizing the garage, or starting that massive home renovation. If your productivity levels are at an all-time low, here's how to tactfully avoid a major household project without sounding like a slacker.

1. **"I've been dealing with a lot of stress lately, and I don't think I can focus on a big project right now. Maybe we can break it down into smaller tasks later?"** Stress is a relatable and legitimate reason to push back on big projects. Offering to break it down into manageable chunks shows that you're still willing—just not *all at once.*

2. **"I've got a busy week ahead, so I'm not sure I'll have the time to start something major. How about we prioritize the smaller things for now?"** Framing it as a time-management issue makes

you sound responsible rather than unmotivated. Prioritizing smaller tasks means you're not totally avoiding work—you're just choosing the easier ones.

3.   **"We might need to plan this out a bit more before jumping in. I'd hate for us to start without being fully prepared."** You're not avoiding the project, you're *strategizing*! Suggesting that more planning is needed buys you time and shifts the focus to preparation rather than execution.

4.   **"I've been feeling really burnt out lately, and I don't think I'll be able to give this project my best effort. Could we postpone it until I'm in a better headspace?"** Burnout is a powerful excuse. By admitting you're not in the right frame of mind, you're showing self-awareness—and that you want to do a good job *when* you eventually tackle the project.

Household chores and projects are a necessary part of life, but that doesn't mean you have to tackle them head-on all the time. Whether it's skipping the grocery run, dodging a repair job, or delaying a big project, these excuses will help you manage your time and energy without letting your household fall apart. With the right excuse, you can prioritize rest, relaxation, or just avoid lifting heavy things—until you're ready (or until someone else does it).

Life throws a lot of unexpected obligations your way, but with these excuses, you'll be able to navigate those moments with ease and grace. Whether it's a knock at the door or a surprise invitation to speak at an event, having a few clever ways to bow out keeps you in control of your time—and your sanity. Remember, sometimes it's okay to say no, and these excuses will help you do it without burning bridges.

www.ingramcontent.com/pod-product-compliance
Lightning Source LLC
Chambersburg PA
CBHW021138260726
48656CB00023B/412